Natural Light

Andrew Peters

TABLE OF CONTENTS

From the Sparkling

Title	Page
String Theory	11
Migration	12
Sails	13
Pelican	14
Rainbows	16
Turtle	18
Hanging Crystal	19
Awakening	20
Autumn	21
Moonlight Sonata	22
Paradigm	23
Dreams	24
Creation	25
Moment	26
Sonnet to Life	27
Human Eyes	28
Bread of Life	30
Welcome	31

In Vivo

Title	Page
High Plains Song	34
Beyond Conversations	35
Hawk	36
Friendship	37
Roundness of Being	38
Swans	42
Sense of Touch	43
Sky and Earth	44
Geese Flying	45
Seed	46
JAZZ	47
Quilting	52
Patience	53
Butterfly	54
Shade	55
Pyramid	56
Eagle's View	57
Lake	58

Whispers in Darkness

Title	Page
Temptation	61
Baptism	62
Brush Fire	63
Blues	64
Until	66
Truth	68
Burning	69
Natural Death	70
Limits	71
Night Comes	72
Gyres	73
Ode to the Western Black Rhinoceros	74
Memorial Day Observance	76
Starry Night	78
Home	79
Bird Feeder	80
Midnight Calls	82
Garden	85

To family and friends
and all who believe in life
and the precious moment

From

the

Sparkling

String Theory

An imperceptible dimension bends:
potential becomes solution;
long-puzzled functions unite
in equivalence; definitions
become words, vibrations
become perceptible.

A twelve-year old views the stream.
The curved hull shifts in rhythm
with the powerful stroke
guiding from the stern.

Just past the thrill of rapids
water finds calm in the deeper route.
The quiet surface reflects
forested banks, the dangling sky.

In wide-eyed, breathless stillness,
sparkles string across the surface.
Rapids are forgotten. The rush
of cascades around the curve ahead
are as yet unheard.

Migration

We live longer than bright mallards
shuffling along shore snatching a meal,
longer than carp leisurely drifting,
waving side-to-side in clear water
under the dock,
not so long as trees lining the shore,
broad-leaved palms open to the sky,
nor as long as this chameleon lake
that may take two generations
to move a limb, or may smile
a hundred times in a single morning.

Webbed feet dangle, visible in clear water
near the dock, mallard swimming
without expectation of morsels,
but quickly learning to wait for more.
It makes mallard sense
to tilt the head back and forth
in search of clues, edging closer
or sidling away as suits the wild need.

Mystery in the green neck shines
off purple feathers interlaced with brown.
Mystery glistens from dark eyes aware,
much as it glistens off algae in the deeps.
Words pronouncing the moment
are as untouchable and fleeting
as each sparkle of light
across the lake's surface.
How agelessly wise, the shining lake
that pulls off shoes and invites toes
to dangle awhile, knowing truth never ends,
but returns as quickly as evening mists,
or as slowly as a season's migration.

Sails

Sails fill with a billowing
like a great heart
        beating
        beating
the pulse of waves between
        shores.

Ah, great creature born
        for wind,
swift in the running,
there are no Cities of Gold.
All beaches speak
answers only varied
by algebraic accents.

Great creature,
swift in the running,
there is only this:
unending wind,
waters teaming with life,
creaking joints,
hazy, sand-rimmed mysteries,
and a long light sparkling
on sharpened waves.

Pelican

Just off shore gliding,
it emerges from the haze up shore.
Wings straight, riding the landward breeze
this way along the coast.

Despite effortless appearance
there is tension in the search
for the flash of movement
beneath white-caps, the deeper catch.

A few gulls follow like courtesans,
hoping for an errant scrap;
their swift darting, sudden changes
of direction seeming arbitrary,
without purpose.

Though gliding briskly, the steady
pelican gaze does not miss a chance:
right there it pulls up,
slows to figure distance,
swings an arch round almost to stop
before the swift, straight plunge.

Waves in endless succession
wash the shore, each rush
proposing an answer.
Holes are filled over;
castles slump and disappear.
Every signifying mark is erased;
every footprint, smoothed.
Wet sand glistens in the setting sun.

The pelican reappears farther on,
continuing down the long coast
and away, just as a group of three
emerge from the haze
headed this way.

Rainbows

Stories of rainbows half-heard
amidst the noise and whirling revelry
of childhood's short-lived innocence
linger into the solitude of night.

Silence, like the darkness,
is but a guess to childhood's incessancy.
Who knows reasons for noise,
or for beliefs which fade
like colors in over-washed cloth?

It's not as if we lost the gleam
of leprechaun's greed
in our eyes, nor dreams of Oz,
nor as if we're freed
of Noah's despair.

Instead, in time, the noise refines
to conversation's art,
and the business of being responsible.
Rainbows when seen at all
cause scarcely a pause
in the rush for silence.
Yet every lull breathes the secret
of just who are the earless
passers-by on whom rainbows are lost.

Belief makes no rainbows:
they appear as a confluence
of serendipitous polarization,
and yet without belief
they are only so much science,
so many means with no ends.

One day myths are myths no more.
Eyes open on a rainbow close by,
not framed at a distance
like paintings half-lit in museums,
but colors cast on moving clouds,
close, so close breathing mingles
with rainbow breath,

gentle as the smell of rainless
           rain.

Turtle

The turtle appeared out of nowhere
like the Bang beginning Time,
discovery of a child, eye to red eye,
unblinking, amazed at a living stone.

Being aware, berries and melon consumed,
the turtle pursued locusts and roaches
with long neck strikes like lightening.

Cool grass across the face
and the shell seals shut.
The carapace is the work of years
layered as strata
or pages of scripture.
Again slow with caution,
the wrinkled neck extends
wisdom familiar to any child.

At last sharp claws carve deep ridges
of patience, perseverance, endurance,
and hope, always hope.
These marks in archetypal earth
form dreams of the world
carried spinning on its back.

But on waking it is just a child
and a turtle, eye to red eye, unblinking,
becoming the integument of time.

Hanging Crystal

Hanging in the window
the prism delights and mystifies
eager children. Pieces of rainbow
scatter flashes that catch
eyes by surprise.

For just that moment,
though unimaginably huge
and hot and distant,
the sun stretches delicate fingers,
tracing the edges
of polished faces.

Awakening

Speechless at the open gate,
wondering how quietly you arrived
in slow spreading colors.

How could you awaken
from endless sleep, blackened cowl
of night and peaceful freedom,
from sleeping to death,
mind evaporating like dry ice?
The creaking gate in the wind
leaves a shuddering.

Now is not mattering why or how.
Yours is the warming course,
silently spinning, carving colors
in the clouds. What matters:
what can be offered in return?

Speechless comes wisdom,
unused to chains of real freedom,
unused to peace surging
like buds pushing up.
Once poet and actor, well-versed,
now speechless watching laughter
in your eyes fill the skies
like stars appearing
one by one, sparkling.

Speechless wonders how dreams
you bring are real,
wonders what to say
to make you stay.

Autumn

The hills unfurl color like grandma
getting down blankets for winter,
time of bare branches silhouetted
at sunset, time of drifting smoke
from hearth-bound homes.

This is poetry written by the sun:
each leaf a line,
each tree a verse,
each hill a volume.

Minds cannot comprehend
the rhymes, the winds
that shift time to memory
and story to silence.

In gathering darkness
unanswerable questions
run like sap to roots,
awaiting the increase of light
and the budding of fresh phrases
growing sunward.

Moonlight Sonata

That moon is gentle
which oversees the sadness
of a night walk,
where home is always
three hours away,
where chimes fade
in the echo of distance.

Darkness allows no memory,
nothing foreseen or planned
in seamless silence.
Footfalls strumming the path
find it plays out midway.

That moon is kind to shine close
to hold the weary traveler
with white-armed consolation,
as though the pathless forest
were home enough,
as though a melody dreamed
might capture the magic of light.

Paradigm

Wild herds gather around the gate,
some nervous, shifting,
others reading or chatting,
settled to await their fate
in the flowing.

Worlds change as easily as
pilots moving the silver dream,
suddenly lifting the head-long
rush over the edge of the world
into invisible rivers,

carrying all the differences
beyond themselves to disappear
among inevitable pathways
to the next reality.

Dreams

They appear like dolphins,
from unfathomed deeps,
at once following and in the lead,
playing in an uncharted course
like children, turning side to side
so the curious eye can see.

Sunlight sparkles across waves,
flashes through the present,
and those bottle-nosed dreams
leap and splash and effortlessly speed,
slapping the surface with wide tails.

This is their divinity:
splashing in currents of memory,
hope rushing through the foam.
Another moment and they disappear
into green depths leaving
the surface its sparkling.

Beyond this brief sail,
through the silver, shining night,
they rise and dive,
following minds
over long curves.

Creation

Drops converge on the pane,
a long stream finding its way
to the ground,

just as from some inner dewpoint,
words congeal to sentences
that find their streaks
through sound.

From the clouds of unknowing,
stories course the generations
to shining pools on cobbled streets.

See the smiling face
among the billows:
feel the overflow spill.

Moment

The waterfall roar overwhelms all other sounds.
Questions hang in the mists.

At the edge the falls mesmerize
those who live beginnings and ends,
who see only the brief drop,
not the patient course of edgeless droplets
winding past trees and slow pools
to this quick rush and beyond.

Understand the chaotic flash,
light finding the tiny drop mid-air,
one individual refraction
for less than a breath's time.

Understand both the single drop
and the billion particle rainbow outlasting
drop after drop, as long as light shines.

Downstream the drop reformed
from mist and foam smooths
a rock face and evaporates.

Sonnet to Life

Supposing the cold deeps of Callisto
move with hungry cells, breathe the breath of life.
Supposing the seas of Enceladus
wake to a living dance of awareness,
impossible microbes stirring darkness.
Perhaps thousands of worlds circle bright stars
in Andromeda, each with forms of life.
Maybe in the time starlight takes to cross

from galaxies beyond, intelligence
of beauty has risen then gone extinct.
A high branch in a nearby maple stirs,
green in translucence against the blue sky.
A warbler hidden in leaves sings, careless.
No moment more worthwhile, none any less.

Human Eyes

The open mouth of a whale descends
on the billions, each krill life
adding less than a second
to that of the whale.

Under the full moon green turtles
emerge from their sandy nests
like D-day in reverse rushing the beach
for the sparkling ocean risking predators
that allow few survivors.

It is human eyes that despair,
watching swirling seasons fly like geese
across the waning moon.
It is the human heart desperate
to postpone endings that invents
wheels and institutions,
the safety of civilization,
marching religions.

In the spring maples and elms
cast seeds by the thousands
spinning and floating in the breeze.
A few find soil, fewer manage roots.
Perhaps but one lives to cast
the next generation.

An owl's talons grasp
what seems to both bird and vole
a significant exchange, life for life,

but from another view,
a subtle shift of energy conserved:
one violin string plucked
begins vibrations in the rest.

It is human eyes that despair,
seeing the storm-weathered nest
and scattered fledglings gasping.
It is the human mind desperate
to know meanings that believes
the future lives in cultivation,
the progress of technology.

It is fear in the eyes
that is blind to the beginning
in every ending.
The last of the salmon lie exhausted,
old scales and fresh roe shining alike
in the shallow rush.

Further up the path the mountain forest
grows less dense. Columns of sunlight
manage straight passage between branches.
Further still past the tree-line
the constant sun and ever-changing winds
come together on the surface
of a high mountain lake
sparkling.

Bread of Life

It begins with a need, hunger,
and a simple decision:
to make bread.

Flour mixes with yeast
and becomes work,
turning and mixing heavy,
thick dough; then, kneading,
here and there sticking to hands,
before smoothness. Work
and time, patience as it rises,
and after more kneading,
rises again.

Baking in the hot oven,
it enters the mind through an aroma
unmistakable in its comforting message,
unyielding in its call to anticipation.

And in the warmth of the bread
on the hands and in the heart,
there is nothing so satisfying
as when it is shared.

Welcome
to my stream of being where the sky
is so blue my eyes hurt with the joyful
knot in my throat from feeling so good
that you are here to see flowers
with me and discuss symmetry
and colors and texture and aromas
and how they might taste if distilled
into jars like strawberry jam and that you
are here to feel warmth of the evening sun
highlighting colors carved through clouds
somehow permeating the crispness of autumn
like a long flame curling around one
of the crosswise logs in the fire we lit early knowing
that darkness will come sometime between
goosebumps and gentle shivering past shades
of red and orange in the sunset which makes us
sigh seeing windows of blue between layers
of clouds which silhouette long black branches
of leafless trees we would know anywhere
but here remind us with a tinge of sadness
of our limitations and distended lives somewhere
crying out from helpless frightened children
until we speak of them and study patterns
in long shadows beneath trees
like lines of our hands foretelling the future
which turns them into symbols of our commitment
focusing our ears on the sounds of our voices
in the silence left by birds sweeping south
until we stop to listen to the crackling hearth
again realizing the amazing intensity
of wonder in each moment moving
to the next which we in awe hardly grasp
at the time except in the roundness
of each other's eyes deeply open
with all senses flowing.

In Vivo

High Plains Song

Where sky is bigger than earth
time slows.   Wind, unaware
of its passage, barely murmurs
over the short grass.
Clouds, like satin robes unfurling
words to verses long lost,
shift sideways, speak their peace
horizon to horizon
and drift on.

In the middle of the wide expanse,
a lizard mounts a changeless rock
looking side to side, hunting.
Lidless eyes blink in the hot sunlight,
in all their living never having seen
life larger than the rock.
And nothing larger has seen
the sharp claws, the quick tongue,
nothing to even speculate
over the meaning of the tilted head.

As far as any eye can see,
even the hawk's circling overhead,
nothing of consequence
to human hearts stirs this dust,
just the life that lives
for itself, the life that doesn't see
itself: the hot flower awaiting
the long-expected rain.

Some unmarked day clouds will gather close,
not to wash what is always clean,
but to repeat their blue story
to tender roots, eager.

Beyond Conversations

Generations of wheat in fields
whisper future generations,
a moving utterance on the wind.

Every animal is the species
repeated, words of ancestors
swirling protein syllables
into elegantly spiraled
nucleic sentences,
conversations of parents
in manifest descent.

Speak in soft tones, then,
and smile gently in the shade.
Listen for the reply
and laugh without knowing why.

Words float like pollen
broadcast on the wind.
They emerge on stems
as glistening fruit.

In the vast airless beyond
the substance of wind,
beyond deep vibrations of time,
feel the intimate story
imagined in the cores of stars
shining like eyes freshly moist.

Hawk

Out-stretched wings hold
the rushing power of the planet
casually while eyes peruse
minute scenes of life and death below.

Below life beats rhythms as of one heart.
Death moves in the shadows
of forgotten moments, imperceptible
to all but those most aware.

A howl rises from mountain forests.
Nervous prey shift quietly
in the long sighs of dust
across distant plains.

The feathered rudder turns
and skims the rim of the wind
across an open field
in silence.

Friendship

In the steepness
where sharp edges bruise
feet and hands in darkness,
and an unsought wind, cold,
scrapes faces, unwanted in the cleansing.
There dawn finds a seedling
impossibly growing from sheer stone.

In that pause of light,
in that wonder of wonders,
friendship appears
in moist eyes that meet,
maybe human,
maybe eyes of elk,
or wolf, or marmot,

most certainly eyes
forever open to the undreamed,
forever ready for the sharing.

Roundness of Being

I

They sit on bleachers baking in the sun,
jostling cold drinks in a gesture towards
the comfort they don't know they have.
Down on the diamond the conflict rages,
tense as a cleated shoe pawing the path,
hanging on the gaze between mound and home.
Then comes the held breath of thousands,
the timeless stretch of a Koufax curve
headed for the zone.

Something about the arch of the ball
and the swing of the bat seems impossible
to straight foul-lines, pointing fingers,
and rays of sun streaming down.

It is a moment not to be forgotten,
not because of the camera shot
in the next-day news.
Rather, it is those there, voices raised
who smell the mustard and bread,
who feel beads of sweat
glisten on their necks
who preserve forever
the path of that curve.

II

Not too far away
the straight drop-back sees
no one open, circling tackles turn
the desperate play into a roll-out
toward the side-line until

just at the last second Unitas
side-winds a perfect spiral
down field, timed perfectly
to hit him at the nine.
The crowd goes wild in heavy coats
yelling their loudest, jumping
higher than the cartwheels of cheers
on the field, clinging to each other
like the long-lost now recovered.

It is a moment not to be forgotten,
though writers of the times
could not describe it well enough
nor find its meaning.
It is the thousands of eyes
there that day that will remember
the perfect arch of the pass
over the shoulder into bent arms.

III

Half a world away stands sway
to unending songs sung in unison.
As one voice, the common is proclaimed,
the Team, enjoined to the well-weighted touch,
the rhythmic, surging dance of the globe.

The struggle on the field rushes back and forth,
swings right and left; each brilliant turn
countered by slide or shoulder, each zipped shot
defeated by smother or fully extended lunge,
until a deft series of one-touch
passing in the eighty-sixth minute
across the field and back
finds Rivellino facing only one,

and leaning left, spins over the ball
creating enough space on the right
for the shot bending, bending,
bending just beyond stretched hands
into the corner of the net,

rippling with the curved rows
of linked arms that will celebrate
evermore the passion and art
of the all-embracing Team.

IV

Off the top of the curved dome,
feverish cheers reverberate,
doubling the sound. Intoxicated
by the aroma of polished wood
and the echoes of past games
hanging from the rafters.
Now they stand. Now they sit
restless, tense as the squeak
of shoes that pivot and cut
impossibilities from wet air.
On the floor, the score climbs point
by point; now one side leads by 5;
now again, they are tied.
This time an alley-oop slam,
the next, a no-look bounce pass
for a lay-up and one for the foul.
The clock winds the tension higher
until as the seconds disappear,

Russell leaps high and fading away
throws up a rainbow that rips the net
as the buzzer ends it there
in graceful memories rising off
hard benches into echoing rafters.

V

Base paths and yard lines, goal posts and benches
speak easy words of linear effects,
irrevocable as time, point to point,
the common language of history.

But there are tongues that speak metaphors
of life beyond the meaning of questions.
Those who hear these ancient songs and poems,
those who perform the roundness of being
reveal the global moment, the beauty
of arching trajectories and curved paths;
the gentle peace as one with bursting joy
of angular momentum, spinning gyres
twisting strings of energy around time,
becoming unforgettably visible.

The experience of momentum touched
ripples in waves of meaning through the dreams
of those who connect foot or hand
to the curve of life, the roundness of being:
waves that roll upon the shore,
air that foils to lift the wing,
planet spinning in curved orbit,
whirling with the wheels of galaxies.

Swans

Swans glide over a dark pool
like the dream of infinite peace.

Rough winds rushing past
elsewhere, here calmly brush
feathered edges, no longer
pushing the future.

Wings lift the gathering.

The curve of them
indelible.

Sense of Touch

The artist begins with a sketch
or two or many more:
potential calculations, vague dreams,
rehearsals unowned by time.

The palette is prepared, paints mixed
and studied, scraped and dabbed.
The moment comes when brush
meets color, carries reality to canvass.

Each bristle a moment, drop by drop
holds the surface long enough
to soak into deeper layers,
artist, idea, canvass, color
forever joined.

Sky and Earth

Thinking
"We are one,"
melt as in warm days
lying in fields of sun.
Backs become sod,
toes and fingers curl in the breeze.
Edges of face and chest
become the open sky.

Roll over and mix sky and earth.

The kiss of eyes,
soft voices caressing ears
mingle together
as a single sigh
and curl in the breeze:
become the deep embrace
of roots to earth.

Geese Flying

Each morning they fly in low
just over housetops in loose
flowing formation gliding
to a nearby pond, scudding
across the dark surface
like so many prodigals returned,
like so many equations
collapsing to zero.

The honking grabs attention,
announcing the future
emanating from beating wings,
perhaps a change of weather
on steep slopes of mountains
half a world away, perhaps
ending unforgiving wars,
or even the malaise
of decadent nations,

perhaps resulting only
in the altered path of a star,
birth of a new universe
when zero achieves division.

In the evening they rise again
flying in low formation
just over housetops away.

Seed

Light soaks into leaves
        like rain to roots,
memories to the surface of time.

Moments spin the spiraled
        web of life,
energy spun nucleic.

Eyes touch the roots of soul,
and hearts hold presence
as a flower holds the seed.

The moment is touched
and spring comes.
The future is born.

JAZZ

Right there, see?
Thirds and fifths, arpeggios,
blue notes and sliding scales,
hoppin' the black keys,
all of it, jazz, see?
Limbs of trees budding out,
fractal as hell, but being no hell,
it's all jazz, see?
like clouds on the horizon moving in
slow as rolling thunder,
sometimes quick as snaps of lightning
billowing out in nimbus dimensions
like flocks of birds,
wings silhouetted against the sky,
calling the flock in trills and lyrics,
all of it jazz,

undulating like ocean surfaces
where the sun touches tips of waves
like fingertips on valves and keys,
delicate or pounding,
depending on mood,
all of it the same but different, see?
because it's jazz,
all of it jazz

language all its own between
math and pure sound and words
and sensations and pure emotion,
taste you never forget,
distant rain in the wind,
fresh as vibrating lips,
because it's jazz, see?
all of it, jazz

sizzling on the wind
like cymbals under the melody
same as fajitas sizzling,
sizzling you taste before you see 'em,
same as jazz, see?
same as out there way out there
where zebra hooves pound out striped rhythms
waiting for elephant trumpets to come in,
but first, winds rush the woodwind strains
through reeds in swamps
then orangutans start swingin' the beat
picked up by rattlers in the Mojave,
ringing through canyons with an eagle solo,
and then there they are, in C major,
elephants right on time
because it's jazz, see?
all of it jazz

reverberating in whale songs
too low to hear, up and down
overtones that catch and hold you
like you're home,
reverberating in the dissonance
of crying babies you have to comfort,
because it's jazz, see?
all of it jazz

bass of a sage grouse on the prairie,
A-flat timed like Billie Holiday
perfectly off beat just enough,
like pi cutting the perfect circle
with the blade of infinite sequences
free as Ornette Coleman
just so you know it's jazz, see?
all of it jazz

decibel vibrations,
earthquake tremors through fault lines,
vigorous hearts beating
same as wavelengths of light,
blue and yellow and red,
green as leaves in spring
with the sun shining through,
all of it jazz,

wavelengths of x-rays
that see through everything,
colors so vivid you're blind,
colors you've never seen,
rainbows on wet streets,
rainbows that follow you,
because it's jazz, see,
all of it jazz

don't think it's just music,
because music is what people do,
write it down, try to repeat it
all over again just the same
like rituals they can remember,
worship even, which is fine,
but jazz is bigger, spontaneous,
it's all jazz, see?

unique as snowflakes filling the sky,
swirling down soft and gentle,
pulling future and past together,
metronome ticking so musicians
have some place to start,
and when they do
jazz comes out,
all of it, jazz

like petals on Fibonacci flowers
Fibonacci in the spirals, too,
horns bent round, the very curve of sound,
more than Satchmo could manage
in the bell of his trumpet,
spilling into vocals that bend
like Einstein's light around stars,
bumpin' and hoppin' in the quantum
here and there at the same time,
there and not there
random as drops of rain
pounding a metal roof faster than Krupa
at the same time planned and figured
depending on the chosen note,
somehow in the right key,
and changing keys,
changing time, cut time,
going on the 5/4,
modulated through blue notes
always blue notes where the soul lives,
because it's jazz, see?
all of it jazz

toes tapping the upbeats,
moves you thought you'd forgotten,
dancing for all you're worth
like excited electrons jumping shells
then losing it to magnetic streams,
jivin' and swingin' in the aisles,
bigger than imagination,
all of it, jazz

big as the moon pulling the sea,
planets that dance the slow unwinding,

big as the macro scale of stars
that know circular breathing
and galaxies that swing and swing
their billion year cycles,
because it's jazz, see?
all of it jazz

loud and fast, volcano explosion loud,
supernova gamma ray burst loud,
have to move loud,
hive of bees dancing
the new fields of flowers dance,
every cell jumpin' hoppin' loud
rollin' over the back loud,
all of it jazz
or soft and gentle,
puffball in a light breeze soft,
single bee on her own far from home,
private grief soft,
staring out rain-streaked windows soft,
meditations calm as a candle flame soft,
because it's jazz, see?
all of it jazz

all of it, all of it jazz,
thirds and fifths, tonic sevenths,
all Stardust in a song, see?
no good and evil,
no past and future,
just beautiful as heaven
right here on earth,
all of it, jazz
all jazz, all of it jazz.

Quilting

Pathways weave through the hills
like thread through mountains
of fabric, scraps spilling
off the table to the floor.

The bridge across the ravine
is the important stitch
leaping the gap,
bringing two sides together.

As evening settles over the woods
like weary hands settling to a lap,
redbirds proclaim their domains
in pieced squares.

Mid-bridge over
invisible boundaries,
see how these woods last
season after season,
beyond moments pouring
through the ravine.

Leaning on the bridge
some truths are thought;
others, felt.
All are woven together like strands
picked up by grandma's hands
continuing the quilt.

Patience

The lioness, eyes half open,
lounges in the hot, sparse shade.
Two wrestling cubs jostle her,
batting her ears, biting her neck.
This is not patience, but tolerance,
the acceptance of what is.

Patience comes later,
crouching in the tall, golden grass,
muscles taut, eyes riveted,
mind calculating,
gauging distance, wind,
geography and time.
Every move measured.
Every breath tuned to the moment,
the all-important moment,
the knot in the weave.
Lion life woven with zebra,
woven with grass, with insects,
with sun, with water.

Aware of hunger and the dangling future,
she moves forward with incalculable care,
sliding through the blowing grass,
smooth as a quantum wave,
the very picture of grace.

Butterfly

Hold it gently in cupped hands,
careful not to tear wings
that smear fine colors on fingers.
Do nothing to hinder flight.

See how wings close tight,
then open wide, flat
with the creation of new stars.
See how antennae move to gather
knowledge and energy,
each twitch a collapse
to an event horizon.

Hold it gently in cupped hands
and share a look among friends.
And at the last open hands
to release precious wings of time,
that the pollen of life
might spread over all the earth.

Shade

Shade circles the back flat, eyes closed.
Breeze ripples hair and clothes.
Light shifts patterns in leaf shadows
sensed inside eyelids.

Spiraling seeds drift by the hush,
some languorous, some rushed,
holding the future like a brush
ready at the canvass.

Beyond the circle, round mouthed sky
blows the broad length of time
through whispering branches pliant
with art grown fresh.

The next thought aware breathes blue.
Eyes open soon on a wider view.

Pyramid

The cold stone has changed little since native
hands wrestled it here breathless
millennia ago. What fear
stacked ton on ton high on this mountain,
seeking permanence?

The sun warms the face, moves shadows
in the valley. There and there,
thin streams of smoke lift life stories
up ever-dissolving columns, spreading
like gyres into ever-widening space.
The presence of spirit
can be smelled far from the fire.
Little wonder these stones are here,
perhaps not from fear at all,
but from views of life down there
going on and on while these slabs
stand centurion to the source of time.
These cold stones see moments
in the valley like heated air
rising above flames,
lifetimes shimmering.

In valley life amid the burning
present, eyes see only fire. But here
past and future twist together
one believable fabric
along the quivering horizon.
Stories carried back become the weave
of baskets and blankets blowing
in the colorful wind, beliefs
understood in patterns of being.

Eagle's View

Rooted to earth the soaring
of an eagle seems impossible,
hanging motionless in the embrace
of the wind, wings tilted at the point
of exact balance.

Imagine the view:
smallest details of fleeting life
running through distant grasses
and purple mists spread
to the farthest limits of sky.

Rooted to earth,
there is no feeling the soft pull
of air ruffling feathers,
no knowing the measure
of unchallenged swiftness.

Details close by are swept up
in a single moment, breathless
on balanced wings,
delicate and strong,
the simultaneous moment,
breathless in the endless present.

Lake

The poetry begins as it always does:
mountain peaks reflected
on a spring-fed surface,
connections made between worlds.

Words, like sharp eyes
are mesmerized by the beauty
of a world they cannot touch,
a world unimpressed by mirrored images,
a world where meaning is judged
by measurable presence.

Scattered scraps flutter like wings
migrating to an unknowable home
where ruffled feathers are smoothed.
Driven by prevailing winds,
see how they swirl and turn,
lifted high, flashing in the sun.

Timeless mountains hold the sky
away from the high lake
long enough for flocks
to gather on the shore,
strutting like they matter,
like they know something.

Sky descends as winter snows return.
Reflections yield to the solidity of ice.
Then the poetry ends as it always does:
dead silence after a brief echo.

Whispers In Darkness

Temptation

Out of deserts whispers arise near,
like sand from winds across plains,
great funnels spinning clouds foretold,
driven in high winds over continents
and oceans around the circling globe.

Dark the clouds appear
though not from cleansing rain.
Some see them as golden;
others, a welcome thought intense.
Some await what might unfold.

Stinging they settle like flocks of fear
hungrily devouring fields of grain.
Some feel from them emboldened,
lifted as on myriad wings the sense
of all that must be told.

For all the art, an end is never clear.
Everything known must be insane
whose purpose passions need control,
caring nothing for what is meant,
but love the ache in endless hollows.

Baptism

Where ice is thick,
forgetting is easy.
Blades dig deeply, cutting intricate figures
on the surface, skating fast.

Cold air in the face takes pain away,
eagerly breathing the deception of freshness,
gliding along, waving to others
at a distance.

Is this peace?   Is it so easy
to forget fear and sorrow?

Darkness comes.   Others stroll away
in small groups, chatting.
Reasons no longer matter.
The thickness of ice doesn't help.

Cold breeze in the face
finally leaves only hollow
absence yearning for warmth
or anything worth the risk
of thin ice

and the touch of clear water.

Brush Fire

Something in the eyes sparks fires
that consume everything,
fields of flame uncontrolled.

Gentler winds clear the air,
smoke drifting for days.
Desolation brings sorrow,
coals flickering in the eyes,
surface of the heart charred black.

From somewhere beyond
sounds of distant thunder
might be forgiveness
moving off or storms
gathering for more.

Leaving is normal, not hearing
sheets of rain move in,
not knowing how green shoots
benefit from prairie fires.

Blues

Smooth as ivory
born of African heat and dust
and jostling herds
that miles later melts
into cool particles
of gently-fingered music,
blue notes echo down city canyons,
off doubled windows
and huge, metal doors,
through putrefied alleys
and off rough concrete corners
and polished granite columns.

Vibrant tones penetrate
mingled mist and soot
and city smoke
deeper than ear-bones,
deep as nucleic voices
singing the atomic songs
of stars.

Luminous as the harmony
of light's droplets rolling
in the great quantum ocean,
blue notes glisten off
long, wet-street nights,
ineffable as the sorrow
of all that is lost,
unstoppable as laughter
effervescing up the glass-paned dark
and into throbbing veins.

The warmth of those tones
moves like ageless howls
across wide deserts
and off mountain peaks,
even down whale-pitched deeps
and up soaring screams of eagles
all condensed to solitary footsteps
echoing off shining pavement.

Now a foot taps worn wooden floors inside.
The singer bends and sways
to notes reverberant,
finds tones pitched between
impossibilities.

Loud as the song of darkness,
this is the soft tone of sorrow.
Wild as wind-whipped leaves
and rumbling hooves,
it is rhythmic as a marathon.
Bold as the half-starved,
this is the dance of fear,
the basic human question.

The whole room breathes

when the music breathes.
Eyes stare at the floor,
following the dim grain
and long cracks,
or at half-empty glasses
adrift with half-melted ice
until
one blue note holds longer.

Until

A million people within the mile.
Crowds in concrete fill the sky
declaring, time-unbounded,
civilization's place.

A million people fill the space
between mirrored walls, move en masse
across plazas of time
as if each bar were a poem,
as if each store were a shrine
whose path to afterlife
is laid on neatly ordered shelves.

Where are you in whose ears
the deeper music moves,
in whose voice the forest
whispers peace.

When are you whose touch
holds petals to stems,
whose melody becomes
the trilled rush through leaves?

Monuments are silent.
A million people scarcely notice
the flash of headlights passing close
to the deep green tomorrow.

And yet in chaos and in silence,
smelling of wet soil and growth,
across fields of time
presence lives unceasing
behind eyes open wide,
forever close dancing
to the dappled music of the sun.

Fields of memories sparkling
in the darkness through spaces
in the clouds invite
the lost millions home
to be at last face to face.

Truth

Truth swims the deepest waters
under sparkling waves.
It soars the highest currents of air
through cloudy veils.
Truth endures harsh deserts,
creates oases of thought.
From every perspective Truth gains
the far sighted view.

Listening, quiet, there is Truth
in forested shade.
Belief is higher up
basking in sun-lit boughs,
but Truth, illusory Truth,
crouching like a tiger,
camouflaged in dappled light,
eyes intent, nostrils flaring,
Truth watches the misled,
listens for mistaken logic,
stretches paws, extends claws
whenever publicists and priests come near.
Take care for those who seek to escape
in the high boughs of belief
find in time the bright light
leaves them blind.

Now and again hunters of Truth
craft heavy nets for a snare,
but when caged and loosed
to study the moving bulge within,
always the net falls open, empty.
Take care for the nose of Truth is keen.
and its sharp teeth in the end
will find us all.

Burning

Those were the care-free days,
green sapling days that pointed
to mysterious futures in the stars.

They were burning even then,
always burning,
every leaf turned to the sun,
every branch swaying
to whispered wind-songs
fresh from distant mountains,
distant shores, distant wide plains.

They were burning even then,
slowly burning, turning carbon
in the fires of living into stems
and knots and the patterned grain
of seasons drenched in rain,
lines and verses
written by rays of light.

Now in greenless days,
days of silent cathedrals
and empty temples,
dry days past summer dreams,
jagged flames ignite,
curving over the curling bark,
lifting brief moments lived

into specks of resurrection,
drifting free at last
in aimless caverns of sky.

Natural Death

Somewhere far away
they climb into jeeps guns ready
for another hunt.
Unsuspecting prey lounge
in the shade.

Here a tiny bird pushed
from a crowded nest struggles
against inevitable fate,
normal sacrifice
for sibling survival.

Thin, undernourished life
still manages a plea.
Here on knees
to find a final rest in the shade,
the weak head leans
against curved fingers.
Beautiful half-formed wings
spread over the trembling palm.

Aware of the noble heart
that fights for precious moments,
how can there be wanton killing
anywhere?

The impression of intricate feathers
and the throbbing chirp
indelibly haunt the privileged mind.

Limits

The old bridge is gone. Weeds
have grown tall near pilings
covered in dank moss that reads
like faded letters of a lost tongue.

Knee deep in the homeless rush,
the mind wanders in dreams
of distances breached,
embankments joined.

Eroded murk feels cold,
pulls at unsure footing,
nothing to hold but slender reeds
waving in the slow current.

To eyes transfixed damp wood glistens
like forgotten myths where heroes
raise from mists the bridge to leap
the chasm as before.

In sober silence, what once was known
almost comes to voice like questions
whispered by the wind to peaks
of waves dissolving into foam.

A shudder, close,
then a long and patient sigh.
Gone, the bridge is gone.

Gulls strut the beach,
angling their everyday beaks
toward scattered scraps.

Night Comes

When night comes along the shore,
waves grow strong, gradual as the song
of the turning moon that says nothing
of darkness, but lifts higher curves
to do their work.

Waves grow strong enough to smooth
the careless sands of their mistakes,
burying flotsam memories
that may have drifted for years but now
find comfort beneath the glistening surface.

Unlike the quiet of forest glooms,
when night comes along the shore
silence gives way to unhushed moans,
as if the very deeps are urged to words
that repeat, repeat inevitable truth,
waves that destroy, waves that resolve,
that blur edges of the knowable present.

When night comes along the shore,
thoughts that strolled the beach before
are left to drift up sunlit streams inland
toward green valleys and snow-capped peaks,
while along the shore edges blur
in bleary fog.

No one wants these thoughtless mists,
hanging like unresolvable hearts:
though they are water for the future,
they arise from lives forever gone,
memories of all that will be missed.

Gyres

Thank you Mr. Yeats for explaining gyres
spinning divergence followed by
convergence
followed by divergence followed by
convergence,

great breath of life, breath of species,
breath of each individual,
in and out breath of God.

But how comes centripetal force
to gather human souls
before the center is lost
to centrifugal myth?

What prods lemmings' rush to cliffs?
What tipping point moves mountain drifts
to avalanche catastrophes?

In this time of divergence,
soul of humanity splitting the world,
axe to logs in preparation,
will it be fire for the hearth
calling convergence anew,
gathered hosts singing songs of old,
telling ancient tales, dreaming new?

Or will this be logs piled upon logs,
set to start the fires of Hell?

Ode to the Western Black Rhinoceros

The vast ocean news
washes over the beach of consciousness
smoothing castles and footprints
and breathing holes, leaving here and there
pebbles and shells, lodged until the next wave
washes them away.
Here's one now:
November 10, 2011
Africa
The Western Black Rhinoceros
has been officially declared extinct by the IUCN.

The myth destroyed itself.
Belief has emptied truth.
The great horn is forever lost
no more the cure it never was.
No more the armored hide shields
every threat but rival horns and human guns.
Few miss the dangerous beast,
the solitary lives unlived.
Fewer still understand what is gone.

The savannahs of West Africa
seem much the same.
The colonies of mites have moved on.
The oxpeckers have found them still.
But in the savannahs of West Africa
there are fewer wallows
to ease the long droughts.
Lions on the prowl are not sniffed out
by acute rhino noses.

The cries of hyenas are no longer heard
by keen rhino ears.
And nowhere in the savannahs
of West Africa are there
four foot horns majestic in profile,
nor any other signs
of the western black rhino.

Far across the ocean news
moves on to arguments over
politics and wars, over
human economies and disasters,
over religious practices.
None of them look for lessons
in the demise of the short-sighted,
irascible western black rhino.

Sadness settles as the dust
across the savannah,
softly,
silently,
dust to dust,
layer upon layer
all too soon becoming
sandstone centuries,
all too soon becoming
the barren planet
that for a brief time
was filled with life.

Memorial Day Observance

I will visit later
after the bands have gone silent.

I will visit later
after the crowds have dried their eyes
and drifted off to backyard grills
and later
to air conditioned entertainment.

I will visit later
after the last words of the proud
have echoed from the farthest rows
of headstones.

Some day some one will say,
"We should gather not in the green season,
but when the ground is cold
and hard, and there are no flowers
and the birds do not sing."

Some day some one will say
"It is enough. There are no more reasons
for wars, no reason for flags,
no reason good enough
to never see you again."

Some day the crowds
will know the real reasons for wars,
the greed of nations,
the arrogant oppression of religions,
the ruthlessness of steaming racism.

I will visit later
when the clouds are like purple ribbon
decorating the horizon.

And I will stay into the darkness
remembering your blue eyes
and the unique curl of hair
over your right temple.

And I will stay as the stars appear
and try to remember
something you said once
that made me laugh.

And I will try to remember
anything that might be more real
than this cavernous feeling
that still loves beyond eternal absence.

Starry Night

At water's edge angled sunlight
glistens across the surface
each small wave a white flash.

The artist knew how light
melts into color, how colors
are blended shade into new shade,
knew how fabric stitches color
to emotion, heart's blood filling
a room with vibrant green and orange.
He understood how time can be cut
like bright yellow flowers
and put in a vase to stand
wordlessly offering hope and joy.

Vincent knew how blue eyes
can see stars spinning
the vast darkness round
in a breathless moment
that once painted
would never be lost.

But also, he knew the knife's edge
that smoothed colors together
could cut flesh and cartilage
hoping for pain less
than the pain of hearing
what no one else hears.

Perhaps it was that moment
he knew what he had to do,
knowing he knew
what no one else knew.

Home

The moon leads on as if home
is found in reflected light.
Maybe it is so.
Who would question the faithful moon
whose ancient myths have shaped
working hands and civilized footsteps?
Who would know that gentle sermon gleam
and not feel hope?

There is a hollow in the moon
deeper than any crater.
Winds moving through it raise
questions of doubt,
words that destroy the essence of home.

Maybe home is lost after all
under the surface there beneath
choppy waves.
Maybe the moon's beacon
is a glittering blade.

The sun, great source of light,
will not be denied its day,
pervasive and offered to all alike.
Maybe there in the horizontal wide
of pinks and reds and purples
and even the constant blue,
maybe there stories enough
will lead the way home.

Or maybe the truth of home
is there in timeless darkness
among trillions of stars.

Bird Feeder

Just another winter for some
        passing
from one great distance
        to another.

They gather in feathered swirls
here at the feeder to chat,
as if this arbor were meant
        only for them.

Unaware of hidden eyes and caring hands,
they rest and eat, ever expecting
        full granaries.
To them, time is but an instinct;
distance, but an urge expressed
        day by day.

They do not know this winter
is like no other.
They can not know
that when their route returns
from warmer, distant climates
en route to other distant moments,
there will be no grain here,
no feeder, no caring hands,
no hidden eyes, brimming with the joy
        of their passing beauty,
full of appreciation
for each of their moments.

They are unaware of the soon vacant house,
unaware of the journey
that ends here, aware only that food
is somewhere else.

From here,
now near the slowing heart,
their distances are not really far,
not nearly so far
as a simple trip
through a vacant house,
not so far as the closing of a door.

Midnight Calls

I

Before advent, fears are small;
pain, a matter of endurance.
Advent begins when endurance ends,
despair that hunger deepens past pain,
that disease ever finds new mediums,
that tyrants never lack for cruelties,
that tragedy and death
lurk at every corner,
at every crossroad chosen.
Advent ends the book,
setting it on the side table,
wondering what comes next,
not hope, but the wait
for the first stars of twilight.

Deep in the center of the night,
time becomes intolerable,
the all-powerful savior,
the dream that vanishes on waking.
Midnight, ignorant of stories,
unaffected by city lights,
knows the end of freedom,
grips the fearful heart,
and renders reins of power
useless as one snowflake
in the avalanche of history.

Comes midnight and parchments fade.
Rituals disappear with the smoke
from abandoned votives.
Comes midnight when myths
that connect stars no longer make sense,
vanities lost in ever-widening darkness.

Little wonder that shepherds,
who leave temples to the faithful,
abandoning sacred stories
for the reality of sheep and predators,
shepherds sure nothing ever changes,
that oppression ever endures,
that freedom is only found afield:
these shepherds watch their flocks
unaware.

II

After every great desolation,
stories of an intervening God
are whispered into new rituals,
scribbled on parchments,
sung into creedal vows so minds
can forget life in favor of easy promises
of an unprovable beyond,
hope in a great return,
hearts beating a unison
that needs no freedom,
no reality that matters.
Such visions create idols
that use belief to justify oppression
and greed and violence.
Leaders arise who misconceive
what it means to be redeemed
when redemption is unneeded.

Whoever would believe,
willing to crawl over sharp edges
of rubble and empty fields,
may yet breathe a fresh breath,
may yet arouse new awareness.

Whoever no longer seeks
a great light finds Messiah
in the light of billions.
Whoever listens in silence
for the voiceless message
will hear whispers of light
coded into every life,
woven into strands of being,
whispers of light in seeds cast wide,
in roots that lead flower to flower unique,
whispers of light in the songs of birds
who sing all they have learned
beyond extinction, survival beyond death.

Such are they who may yet taste the bread
of a paradise that was never lost,
that lives only on earth.
Such are they who have heard
the message that begins "fear not,"
and beats blades of swords
into compassion for the poor and weak.
Such are they who hear truth that needs
no angel chorus, no kings,
no violence to find peace,
no words to understand beauty.
Such are they who may yet hear
justice as simple as a baby's breath,
as difficult as God crucified.
Such whispers of light need no creeds
to become lives unafraid of death,
lives aware of peace.

Garden

The sounds are everywhere.
No longer a gentle hum in the distance
like trucks on a highway maybe,
now up close everywhere.

Shining in the sun, the great machine
grinds through the earth
piling city upon city,
ignoring previous rubble.

Amid all other discoveries,
now, perhaps too late, there is this:
this has been the garden all along:
not expulsion, rather abdication.

And now, fresh breeze turned stale,
all the selves having been found
are lost,
forbidden fruit found at last.

High up, a flash of red wings precedes
cardinal proclamation among the leaves.
Somewhere, like memories undreamed,
it sounds like the blues come echoing.

Heaven, beautiful as ever,
shudders softly
on the way out.

www.ingramcontent.com/pod-product-compliance
Lightning Source LLC
Chambersburg PA
CBHW051409290426
44108CB00015B/2217